**W9-AMO-346**

Getting To Know...

Nature's Children

PELICANS

Candace Savage

PUBLISHER	Joseph R. DeVarennes
PUBLICATION DIRECTOR	Kenneth H. Pearson
MANAGING EDITOR	Valerie Wyatt
SERIES ADVISOR	Merebeth Switzer
SERIES CONSULTANT	Michael Singleton
CONSULTANTS	Ross James
	Kay McKeever
	Dr. Audrey N. Tomera
ADVISORS	Roger Aubin
	Robert Furlonger
	Gaston Lavoie
EDITORIAL SUPERVISOR	Jocelyn Smyth
PRODUCTION MANAGER	Ernest Homewood
PRODUCTION ASSISTANTS	Penelope Moir
	Brock Piper

EDITORS

Katherine Farris	Anne Minguet-Patocka
Sandra Gulland	Sarah Reid
Cristel Kleitsch	Cathy Ripley
Elizabeth MacLeod	Eleanor Tourtel
Pamela Martin	Karin Velcheff

PHOTO EDITORS	Bill Ivy
	Don Markle
DESIGN	Annette Tatchell
CARTOGRAPHER	Jane Davie
PUBLICATION ADMINISTRATION	Kathy Kishimoto
	Monique Lemonnier

ARTISTS

Marianne Collins	Greg Ruhl
Pat Ivy	Mary Theberge

This series is approved and recommended by the Federation of Ontario Naturalists.

DB GF DB BB DS FP OK manor

Canadian Cataloguing in Publication Data

Savage, Candace, 1949-
  Pelicans

(Getting to know—nature's children)
Includes index.
ISBN 0-7172-1930-5

1. Pelicans—Juvenile literature.
I. Title. II. Series.

QL696.P47S38 1985   j598.43   C85-098727-X

Have you ever wondered . . .

933400

Before you start reading about pelicans, here is something for you to do. Get a piece of paper and something to draw with. Now draw a bird. Make it the strangest bird you can imagine. Remember to give it a head, two eyes and a beak, a body, two wings and two legs. Be sure to give it feathers too. Otherwise it won't look like a bird.

Now compare your imaginary bird with the pictures of pelicans in this book. Which is stranger?

When you are deciding, think of this: pelicans really exist. Don't you think that makes them strangest of all?

Brown Pelican.

A Pod of Pelicans

As soon as it can climb out of the nest, a young pelican looks for other birds its own age. At first, the youngsters just get together during the day, each returning to its own nest at night when one of its parents comes back to keep it warm. But later on, the young birds spend all of their time in groups.

The youngsters in these groups, called pods, often do things together. They are just like flocks of sheep. If one bird moves into the shade, dozens follow. If one goes to the shore, a hundred others tag along behind.

If they are badly frightened by a boat, a low-flying airplane or a person, the youngsters rush together in a squirming, wriggling mass, sometimes crawling right over top of one another as they all try to hide in the center of the pack.

Three-week old Brown Pelican chick.

Pelicans Here and There

There are actually six different kinds of pelicans in the world today, at least one on every continent. All pelicans are water birds and are usually found around rivers, lakes and oceans.

In North America, there are two kinds of pelicans. The Brown Pelican lives on the sea coasts of the southeastern and western United States. The White Pelican nests mostly on lakes in western Canada and the western United States.

The pelican folds its enormous pouch under its bill when not using it.

Browns and Whites

It is easy to see how the two North American pelicans got their names. As you might expect, the Brown Pelican is mostly brown, but it has silvery gray streaks and white markings on the underside of its wings. The White Pelican is almost pure white, except for dark wingtips.

Both pelicans are easy to spot in the air or in the water. They fly with their head pulled back and their bill pouch resting lightly on their chest. In the water they float high because of air trapped in their feathers and air sacs under their skin.

In order to waterproof itself, the pelican regularly preens and oils its feathers, using oil collected from a gland at the base of its tail.

Two Homes

Pelicans that nest in northern areas where winters are cold often have two homes. In the fall, when chilly winds begin to blow and the temperature drops to near freezing, they leave their nesting grounds and head south in search of a friendlier climate.

Some pelicans must fly hundreds of kilometres (miles) between their summer nesting grounds and winter feeding grounds. The journey is called migration. Fortunately pelicans are well equipped for long-distance flying.

The pelican's powerful wings can carry it through the air at over 40 kilometres (25 miles) per hour.

Heavy Flyer

One of the most impressive things about pelicans is their size. They are among North America's largest birds.

Adult White Pelicans sometimes weigh more than 10 kilograms (22 pounds). That is about as much as a large turkey. Brown Pelicans are slightly smaller.

Because they are so heavy, pelicans often have to work hard to get into the air. Like airplanes, they always take off into the wind. If there is no wind, they get up speed by running across the surface of the water, beating their wings and pumping their feet as they go. When they are traveling fast enough, they rise into the air.

There is nothing graceful about a pelican landing. They often plop down with a splash, sometimes with their feet stuck out in front of them to act as brakes.

Lift-off.

Lots of Wing Power

Pelicans have long, wide wings. How long? To find out, get a ruler and measure two and a half metres (8 feet) on the floor. That is how far an adult White Pelican's wings will reach when they are stretched out. Some pelicans' wings stretch even wider.

Once they are in the air, pelicans fly with grace and strength, thanks to their powerful wings. Sometimes they flap their wings; other times they glide on rising currents of warm air. When they glide, it seems magical to see their heavy bodies sailing, silent and motionless, through the sky. They can ride up on the air currents, higher and higher until they are tiny specks.

Brown Pelicans will fly long distances in search of food.

A Flock of Flyers

Pelicans usually fly in flocks. In
fact, they do almost everything in
flocks. They are very social birds.

Often they travel one behind the
other in a long line. Sometimes,
they fly in a wide "V." Their
wing beats are slow and dignified:
flap, flap, flap and g-l-i-d-e. Each
bird takes its cue from the one in
front of it, so that they either
move their wings at the same time
or one after the other. Often the
flapping motion seems to pass
down the line like a wave.

Sky Fishers

Brown Pelicans even fish from the sky. This is not as strange as it sounds. What they do is dive head first into the ocean and catch fish swimming just below the surface in their bills. Usually they plunge down from a height of about seven metres (23 feet). They plan their dives carefully so that they end up exactly where the fish are.

Fortunately, crashing into the water from high in the air does not hurt them. Air trapped in pockets under the skin and between their feathers helps to cushion the force of their dive.

Brown Pelicans catch small fish that live in schools such as pigfish, pinfish, sheepshead and silversides.

A Brown Pelican dives for its meals.

The Brown Pelican relies on its sharp eyesight to help it locate fish beneath the surface of the water.

Sly Fishers

White Pelicans are fish-eaters, too, but they do not make spectacular dives to catch their dinner like the Brown Pelicans do. Instead, they dip their beaks (and sometimes their heads) underwater as they swim along and scoop up their food. They eat whatever is easiest to catch: minnows, perch, suckers, carp and sometimes frogs or salamanders.

When they are fishing in deep water, White Pelicans usually feed alone. But when they are in the shallows, they often work together.

Here is how they do it. A number of pelicans paddle around, not seeming to pay much attention to one another. But the instant a school of fish swims among them, the birds form a ring around it. They move in slowly, herding their prey toward the center. Then, when the fish are packed together in the center of the circle, the pelicans begin to feed in a wild free-for-all of jabbing beaks and splashing feet. Each bird gets a bigger meal than it would have by fishing on its own.

Opposite page:

White Pelicans fishing for dinner.

A Handy Scoop Net

Pelicans have a special tool that they use for fishing. Can you think what it might be?

If you guessed their famous beak with its attached pouch, then you are right. The beak and pouch serve as a dip net. The pelican dips its beak into the water and scoops up a pouchful of water. If it is lucky, there will be some fish in the water too. When its pouch is full, the pelican squeezes out the water and swallows the fish whole.

The pelican's pouch is so stretchy that it can hold more than 10 litres (just under 10 quarts) of water and fish. How much is that? To find out, put the stopper in the kitchen sink. Then get a one-litre (1-quart) milk carton, fill it with water and empty it into the sink. Do that 10 times and you will know how much a pelican's pouch can hold.

In spite of what you may have heard about the pelican, its bill will not hold more than its belly can.

Big Mouth

You have probably seen cartoons that show pelicans flying and walking with things in their beaks. In real life, pelicans do not do this because their beaks are not made for carrying things.

If you put something in your pocket, you can be pretty sure it will stay there because your pocket has a bottom. But a pelican's pouch is really just a stretchy tube that empties into its throat. As soon as the bird lifts its head, the fish in its pouch slide down its throat into its stomach.

Pelicans' throats and stomachs are stretchy too. When fishing is good, the birds stuff themselves to the very brim. They often eat several hundred minnows, about three and a half kilograms of them (8 pounds), at a time. Sometimes they pack in so much they cannot even get airborne. They have to throw back part of their catch in order to take off.

Air Conditioned Pouches

Fishing is not the only way in which pelicans use their pouches. They also use them as a way of keeping cool. How?

Have you ever noticed a dog on a very hot day? What does it do with its tongue? It sticks it out and breathes fast, or pants. When the dog pants, air moves over the moist surface of its tongue and the dog cools off. Try it yourself. Does your tongue feel cool?

When a pelican is very hot, it flutters the moist skin of its pouch so that air moves around it. How do you think this makes the pouch feel?

Keeping cool.

933400

Pelican Talk

Believe it or not, pelicans also use their pouches to help them communicate with one another.

When two White Pelicans meet each other, they sometimes puff out their pouches, point their beaks straight up and turn their heads slowly from side to side. This is the pelicans' way of saying hello.

Web-Footed Friends

If you spent as much time in the water as a pelican does, you would want to wear flippers to help you get around. A pelican does not need flippers. Its feet are already webbed to give it lots of paddling power.

Unfortunately webbed feet are not always a help. On land they can be a bit of a nuisance, as you will know if you have ever tried to walk anywhere in flippers. A pelican on land throws its body from side to side and waddles awkwardly. Quite a change from its graceful fast-speed swimming style.

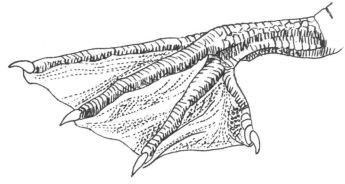

Pelican foot.

Courting Time

Brown Pelicans mate at various times during the year, depending on where they live, while White Pelicans mate in late spring. But before a pelican can mate, it must choose a partner.

Pelicans try to attract a partner by performing a courtship "dance." This is not like any dance that people do. Sometimes a male pelican will stomp in a flat-footed way around a female. Other times the male will strut around and bow as if to say: "Don't you think I am handsome."

Like many birds, White Pelicans also put on their brightest colors to attract a mate. But they wear their bright colors on their pouches. For most of the year, a White Pelican's pouch is a dull yellow-orange, but in spring it turns bright orange. At the same time, the birds grow a furry bump, or horn, on their bills. Some also grow a pale yellow crest on their heads and pale yellow chest feathers.

The strange bumps on this bird's beak indicate that it is mating season for White Pelicans.

Quite a Crowd

White Pelicans always make their nests on islands, usually far out in lakes. This keeps their eggs safe from hungry predators and away from people. Brown Pelicans often nest on islands too. But they will choose other nest sites if they seem safe. If you come across a pelican nest, it is very important to stay away from it. By going close, you may upset the pelican parents and make them leave their nest. When that happens, the young pelicans often die.

Pelicans do not nest alone. Hundreds of them nest together in colonies. A pelican colony is a messy, crowded place. The ground is covered with bird droppings and rotting fish, so you can imagine how it smells.

As many as 1000 pairs of pelicans may gather together in a nesting colony.

Sticks and Stones

Nest building is easy for a White Pelican. It simply sits on the ground and turns round and round, dragging its bill as it goes. It pulls earth, twigs and small stones into a saucer-like ring as it turns. Presto—a nest!

Brown Pelicans put a bit more work into building their nests. The pelican pair gather sticks and make a platform with a hollow in the middle for the eggs.

When the nest is ready, the mother pelican lays two or three eggs. For a whole month, the parents take turns sitting on their eggs. Like other birds, pelicans have to keep their eggs warm so that the young can grow inside them.

Taking the afternoon egg-sitting shift.

Is It a Bird?

When a baby pelican first crawls out of its shell, it looks more like a reptile than a bird. It is pink-skinned and featherless and so small and weak that it can scarcely raise its head. At feeding time, its parents dribble food into its tiny mouth from the tip of their huge beaks.

But come back a month later and you will see a much different scene. The young pelican is now much bigger and covered in thick, white down. It can walk, in a teetering, tottering, toddler sort of way, tripping over nothing and often falling down.

A hatchling only a mother could love!

A Hungry Horde

Young pelicans leave the nest and join a pod of other youngsters before they are able to fly or feed themselves. But their mothers and fathers do not forget them. They drop by to feed the young birds several times a day.

When an adult arrives, the young pelicans in a pod act as if they are starving to death. They peck at the adult's feet, reach for its bill, even climb up its body. One or two may seem to go crazy: they fling themselves on the ground, flap wildly and wave their heads back and forth. They may twirl round and round, growling and biting their wings. This is their way of saying "Feed me! Feed me!"

Would you like to have lunch by reaching into your parent's throat for a mouthful of half-digested fish? Probably not, but young pelicans enjoy feeding in this way. In fact, they often will not remove their heads from their parent's throat when the adult wants to leave. Sometimes, they have to be shaken loose!

Opposite page:

Pelican parents will only feed their own young. No one knows how they recognize them amid the mass of clamoring chicks, but they do. The young know their parents, too.

First Flight

By the time they are about three months old, young pelicans are ready to try flying. Take-offs and landings are especially difficult at first. They awkwardly blunder up into the air and then belly flop into the water. But practice makes perfect and soon they are flying confidently. By the fall, young pelicans that live in cold climates are strong enough to join the adults on the long flight south to their winter feeding grounds.

The young pelicans do not get their full adult feathers until they are a year old. Then, they look just like their parents. But although they *look* grown-up they are not yet ready to raise their own families. That will not happen until they are three or four years old.

By the time this young pelican leaves the nest, it will have consumed about 70 kilograms (150 pounds) of fish!

The Final Chapter

So now you have the whole story of pelicans. Think about all the surprising things you have discovered:

- how many different kinds there are and how big they can get;
- how some can dive into the ocean and catch fish with their pouch nets;
- how they use their pouches to cool off and to talk to one another;
- how they nest in busy colonies and grow up in groups;
- how the young dance and carry on when they are begging and reach right inside their parents' mouths for food!
- how long it takes them to grow up.

The more you learn about pelicans, the more wonderful they become.

Special Words

Colony The nesting site where hundreds of pelicans lay their eggs and raise their young.

Courtship The process of attracting a mate.

Crest Tuft on a bird's head.

Digestion The process by which swallowed food is broken down by stomach juices so that the body can use it.

Display A special pattern of behavior many birds use as a means of communication.

Down Very soft, fluffy feathers.

Mate To come together to produce young. Either member of an animal pair is also called the other's mate.

Migration Traveling at regular times in the year in search of food or a place to nest and raise young.

Pod A group of young pelicans.

Reptile Class of animals that includes lizards, snakes, turtles, alligators and crocodiles.

Webbed feet Feet in which the toes are joined together by flaps of skin.

INDEX

Cover Photo: Stephen J. Krasemann (Valan Photos)

Photo Credits: J.D. Taylor (Miller Services), page 4; W. Metzen (Miller Services), pages 7, 44; Camerique (Miller Services), page 8; Wayne Lankinen (Valan Photos), pages 12, 15, 24, 32, 36, 39, 43; Stephen J. Krasemann (Valan Photos), pages 11, 23, 27, 31; FPG (Miller Services), page 16; Dennis Schmidt (Valan Photos), page 19; George Peck, pages 20, 28, 40; Tom W. Hall (Miller Services), page 35.

Getting To Know...

Nature's Children

SNAKES

Merebeth Switzer
and
Katherine Grier

PUBLISHER	Joseph R. DeVarennes	
PUBLICATION DIRECTOR	Kenneth H. Pearson	
MANAGING EDITOR	Valerie Wyatt	
SERIES ADVISOR	Merebeth Switzer	
SERIES CONSULTANT	Michael Singleton	
CONSULTANTS	Ross James	
	Kay McKeever	
	Dr. Audrey N. Tomera	
ADVISORS	Roger Aubin	
	Robert Furlonger	
	Gaston Lavoie	
EDITORIAL SUPERVISOR	Jocelyn Smyth	
PRODUCTION MANAGER	Ernest Homewood	
PRODUCTION ASSISTANTS	Penelope Moir	
	Brock Piper	
EDITORS	Katherine Farris	Anne Minguet-Patocka
	Sandra Gulland	Sarah Reid
	Cristel Kleitsch	Cathy Ripley
	Elizabeth MacLeod	Eleanor Tourtel
	Pamela Martin	Karin Velcheff
PHOTO EDITORS	Bill Ivy	
	Don Markle	
DESIGN	Annette Tatchell	
CARTOGRAPHER	Jane Davie	
PUBLICATION ADMINISTRATION	Kathy Kishimoto	
	Monique Lemonnier	
ARTISTS	Marianne Collins	Greg Ruhl
	Pat Ivy	Mary Theberge

This series is approved and recommended by the Federation of Ontario Naturalists.

Canadian Cataloguing in Publication Data

Switzer, Merebeth.
  Snakes

(Getting to know—nature's children)
Includes index.
ISBN 0-7172-1929-1

1. Snakes—Juvenile literature.
I. Title. II. Series.

QL666.06S97 1985   j597.96   C85-098738-5

Have you ever wondered . . .

When you see a snake gliding through the grass or basking on a warm rock, what do you feel?

People often feel strongly about snakes. In many stories, snakes are portrayed as villains. But different kinds of stories have also been told.

Long ago the Greek people saw that snakes shed their old worn skins to reveal a fine new skin beneath. They thought of this new skin as a sign of life and health. Doctors today still use a picture of two snakes curling up a staff as the sign of their profession.

One thing is certain. Snakes have been misunderstood. What are snakes really like? Only careful watching can tell. You can begin yourself. And naturalists who study snakes can tell us much more about how they live and how they are suited for the role they play in the natural world.

Scaly Relatives

Snakes are reptiles. So are lizards, turtles, alligators and crocodiles. That means that they are covered with tough, dry scales rather than fur or feathers. Their young usually hatch from eggs. They breathe air into lungs. And, unlike people, they have no built-in temperature control. Their temperature is affected by the temperature of the air, water or earth around them. In these ways, all reptiles are the same.

But in other ways snakes are different from their reptile relatives. How? One big difference is easy to see. Snakes do not have legs. A few still have small bones and a claw left where their ancestors had hip and leg bones, but these leg leftovers do not help the snake move.

Why don't snakes have legs? Scientists think that long ago, snakes' lizard-like ancestors began to hunt for food in other animals' burrows. But their legs got in the way in such narrow spaces. Very gradually their legs disappeared so that snakes could hunt more successfully underground.

Opposite page:

The Northern Red-bellied Snake is usually active at night.

6

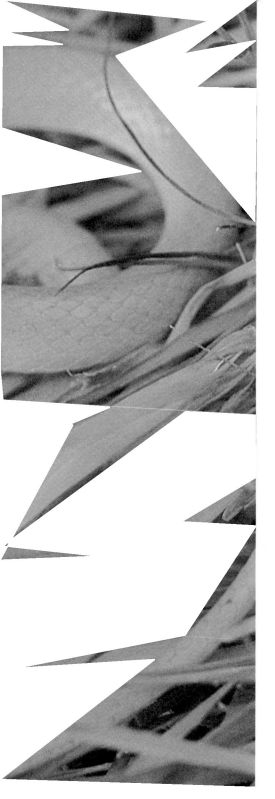

Snakes, Snakes and More Snakes

About 320 different kinds of snakes live in North America. They need food, water, warmth and shelter to live. They find these in many different kinds of places. Some snakes live in deserts while others live in forests, grasslands or mountains. Some spend much of their time burrowing underground, and others live almost entirely above ground. There are snakes almost everywhere in North America and the rest of the world, except in the far north where the winters are very long and cold. There are no snakes in Iceland, Ireland and New Zealand.

The beautiful Smooth Green Snake is rarely seen because it blends in so well with the surrounding greenery.

Long and Slim

Some snakes are huge. The largest snakes in the world can grow as long as five men lying head to toe. But in North America, the largest snakes only grow as long as a man is tall. The shortest is about the length of a new pencil. Most are somewhere in between.

Big or small, a snake's basic shape is the same—long and slim. The snake has many organs that are almost the same as yours, doing the same sorts of jobs: breathing in air, pumping and cleaning the blood, taking the nourishment from food and getting rid of what is left.

But how do all those organs fit? They become long and slim just like the snake's body. And if there were once two organs of one kind, one has shrunk or disappeared completely.

Occasionally snakes are born all black instead of their regular color. This Garter Snake is hard to recognize without its stripes.

A Skin of Scales

A snake's skin is made up of many scales. There are small scales on its back and sides and larger ones on its head. Running from head to tail along its belly is a row of big rectangular scales called scutes.

A snake's scales look like separate pieces of skin, but they are not. The snake's outer skin is all one piece. In between the scales, there are hidden folds of skin that join each scale to the next one. These folds let the skin stretch as the snake curves its body or swallows a large meal.

A snake has three layers of skin. The inner one holds the snake's colors and patterns. The middle one is like a factory, always building the outer layer. The outer layer is transparent and hard and thin. It is made of the same substance as your fingernails and protects the snake from rough objects as its moves along the ground. This outer skin even covers the snake's eyes, like a clear bubble. In fact, the eyes are protected by this layer of skin instead of by eyelids that close. That is why a snake's eyes are always open, even when it is asleep.

Opposite page:

You can tell the Garter Snake is active during the day by its round pupils. Snakes that move at night have slit-like pupils similar to a cat's.

Changing Skins

You lose tiny flakes of old skin every day, but a snake sheds its old outer skin all in one piece. Shedding its skin is important for a snake.

Young snakes need room for their growing bodies, but their outer skins never grow. So they must grow new, larger ones, usually about six times a year. Older snakes do not grow as fast, but their skins get worn with use. They shed a few times a year.

A snake's old skin must separate from the new one before it can be shed. A milky liquid builds up under the outer skin and loosens it. It even covers the snake's eyes so that it cannot see very well. A few days later the snake rubs its nose against a twig and makes a break in the old skin. Then it slithers out of it, peeling it off inside out as you would pull a sweater over your head.

The old skin is clear but it shows the outline of every scale and the folds of skin in between. The new skin is fresh and shiny, and the snake's colors and patterns show up more brightly than ever through it.

Garter Snake shedding its skin.

Opposite page:

An Eastern Milk Snake about to shed. Note the foggy eye.

No Arms, No Legs—But Can They Move

Think for a moment of the parts of your body you use when you walk, run or swim. It is hard to imagine moving without arms and legs, isn't it? But a snake does not have arms or legs—or fins or wings. How, then, can it move so easily and gracefully?

The snake has a backbone that runs from the base of its head to the tip of its tail. This backbone is made up of many small bones that are all connected. Each one can move slightly sideways and up and down. These bones let the snake curve back and forth.

But a snake's bones could not go anywhere without the muscles that are attached to them. A snake moves by tightening or relaxing its muscles, just as you do. The muscles pull or push the bones so that the snake's whole body moves forward. To help move itself along, the snake grabs on to twigs or rocks or bark with its belly scales. They give the snake its grip and keep it from slipping backwards.

Opposite page:

Coiled and ready to strike. (Pacific Rattlesnake)

Different Places, Different Moves

Just as you can, a snake can move in several different ways. It can wriggle forward, curving its body into an S. In water or on land, this is the way most snakes travel.

Or a snake can side-wind. The snake curves its body into loops and throws each loop sideways, clear of the ground. Snakes use side-winding in shifting sand where scutes cannot get a good grip. And because only the bends of each loop touch the ground, many snakes side-wind if they are moving across hot sand.

A snake can also push and pull itself up trees or along narrow passages. First it curves the front half of its body into tight loops and grips with its front scutes. Next, it pulls the back half of its body forward into new loops and takes hold with its rear scutes. Then it begins all over again.

Milk Snake.

Finally, a snake can creep along in an almost straight line. For a long, heavy snake this is much easier than weaving from side to side. Its muscles lift and pull a scute ahead. The scute grips the ground where it lands. Then the muscles move the next scute ahead and the next and the next. The muscles pull the snake's body forward bit by bit.

Most snakes have one favorite way of traveling, such as side-winding. But many use a combination of moves. For example, a heavy snake that usually creeps forward in a straight line can use the wavy S if it needs to move fast.

You might think that snakes move easily only on land, but most snakes can also swim if they have to. Some water snakes even hunt for food in the shallows of lakes and rivers and swim long distances across open water.

Even though a water snake spends a great deal of time searching for food in ponds and lakes, it sleeps on dry ground.

Snake Sense

Using its heat sensors, a viper and some other snakes can hunt and strike in total darkness.

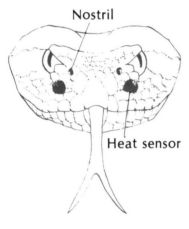

Nostril

Heat sensor

You learn about your world by seeing, hearing, touching, smelling and tasting it. Snakes learn about their world a little differently.

Snakes' eyes and ears do not work the way yours do. They cannot see very clearly or tell how far away things are. And snakes do not have ears like yours with eardrums that pick up sounds carried by air. So when a snake charmer plays a flute, the snake does not hear a sound. It sways to the charmer's movements, not his music.

But a snake's eyes can spot tiny movements. And it has inner ears that pick up vibrations from the ground.

A snake's sense of touch is more like yours. Although its skin is scaly, it can feel all over. And many snakes that prey on warm-blooded animals have special heat sensors that tell them if something warm—and maybe good to eat— is nearby.

Sidewinder.

A Tongue with a Difference

Although a snake learns a lot about its world through vibration and touch, it learns most by using its tongue. A snake's tongue is long and forked at the end. It can hardly taste things at all, but it *can* smell things. How?

If you watch a snake you will see that it is always darting its tongue in and out of its mouth. The tongue picks up tiny bits of scent information from the air and the ground. When the snake pulls its tongue back into its mouth, it puts the forked tips into two small holes in the roof of its mouth. These holes work just like your nose. They send signals to the snake's brain to tell it what it has "smelled" with its tongue.

Garter Snake.

Skilled Hunters

All snakes, big and small, are meat-eaters. But they catch their prey in different ways. Some catch and hold their prey with their teeth before eating it live. Some are constrictors. They coil around their prey and squeeze it so it cannot breathe. And others poison their catch by spurting venom into it through long, hollow fangs. The venom is made in a small venom gland at the back of the mouth.

Once a snake has caught its prey, it eats it whole. It cannot do anything else. It does not have sharp cutting teeth or flat chewing teeth. Its teeth are pointy and curved inward and good for holding onto its prey.

Depending on its size, a snake eats insects, frogs, mice, rats, other snakes, larger animals or the remains of other hunters' kills. Often a snake eats a meal several times bigger than its mouth.

These fangs will swing outward when the snake attacks and pull back into their sheaths when the snake closes its mouth.

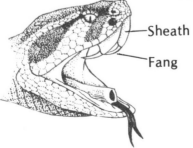

Sheath

Fang

This Pacific Rattlesnake has taken over a magpie nest.

Super Swallowers

Imagine trying to swallow an apple whole. Could you do it? Of course you couldn't. So how can a snake swallow something larger than its own head? To a snake, big mouthfuls are not a problem. Its jaw bones can separate from the rest of its skull and from each other to stretch open. The bottom jaw bones even split in the middle. Now the snake has a huge mouth and no bones to get in the way.

But even with such a big mouth, swallowing is a slow business. Bit by bit, the snake works its jaws around its prey. Soon its throat starts to tighten and pulls the animal into the snake's stomach. Before long there is no sign of the prey—except for a bulge moving slowly down the snake's body.

A snake that has swallowed a big meal may take days or even weeks to digest all of it. During that time it will not need to eat anything else.

As its name suggests, the Blue Racer can move very quickly when it wants to.

Avoiding Danger

Snakes have many enemies in the natural world—meat-eating birds and animals, some reptiles and even other snakes.

Some snakes have colors and patterns that help them hide from their enemies. For example, it is difficult to see a green snake among leaves or grass, or a mottled black and brown snake among rocks or sand. Other snakes are brightly colored. Many of them are very poisonous. Some people think that their bright colors warn their enemies that they are dangerous.

When a snake senses danger, the first thing it does is try to get away. If it cannot flee, it tries to protect itself.

The Southern Ring-necked Snake is also known as the "corkscrew" snake.

Defense Tactics

Some kinds of snakes try to scare their enemies away. They hiss or rattle their tails or puff themselves up so they look big and ferocious. Others give off a smelly, terrible-tasting musk if they are picked up. And some even roll over and pretend to be dead.

A few snakes are quick to attack. But most strike only if they cannot escape or scare off their enemies. The weapons they use to defend themselves are the same ones they use for hunting. Some bite, some use venom and some try to squeeze their enemies so they cannot breathe.

A rattlesnake's tail has several horny rings that rattle against each other when the snake shakes it. The sound is a warning not to be ignored: "Back off or else!" (Western Diamond Rattlesnake)

33

Too Hot? Too Cold?

You are warm-blooded. This means your body automatically controls its own temperature so it stays much the same no matter how hot or cold the weather is.

Snakes are cold-blooded. Their bodies do not control their temperature as ours do. If it gets cold out, the snake's temperature drops. If it gets hot, so does the snake. But snakes like the same range of temperature we do— T-shirt weather. That is when their bodies work best and they are alert and agile.

Snakes must control their temperature by moving to places where it is warmer or cooler. A snake warms itself by basking in the sun out of the wind. It can cool itself by seeking shade or wet shorelines or by going undergound.

Big snakes do not live in cool climates. It would be too hard for them to keep warm. Many snakes that do live where it is cooler are brown or black. Their dark colors take in the sun's warmth much faster than lighter colors and help them keep warm.

Opposite page:

Small Brown or De Kay Snake

Overleaf:

The Hog-nosed Snake is a great bluffer. When threatened it spreads its neck like a Cobra, opens its mouth and hisses, but it has never been known to bite.

Away from Winter's Chill

How do snakes in cold-weather country
survive winter? As the days grow shorter and
colder, snakes move more and more slowly
and become less and less alert. When it is too
chilly for them to warm themselves by lying in
the sun, they must look for shelter. They need
protection from freezing weather and from
alert, warm-blooded enemies.

A snake's winter shelter is called the snake's
hibernaculum. A crevice in rocks, a space
beneath a log or an animal's underground
burrow will all serve as a hibernaculum.

Once it has found shelter, the snake
hibernates for the whole winter. Its heart beats
more slowly. It breathes less often. And
because it stays still, it uses so little energy that
it does not need to eat again until spring.

Some snakes hibernate alone, but a large pit
or burrow can attract many snakes. Different
kinds of snakes and sometimes even enemies
will pass the winter side by side. Once a snake
has found a shelter, it will return to the same
place year after year.

Opposite page:

*Cluster of
rattlesnakes.*

Spring Mating

As the spring days grow warmer and longer, snakes that have spent the winter hibernating wriggle out of their shelters. The warm weather tells them that now is the time to mate. The male finds the female by following the scent she leaves on the ground. Snakes often mate with different partners during mating season.

Sometimes two males pretend to fight to decide which one will mate with a female. They lift their heads, twist their bodies together and try to upset each other's balance. But they do not bite or hiss. Eventually the weaker snake leaves.

The Kingsnake is truly the king of snakes. It can attack even poisonous rattlesnakes since it is not harmed by their venom.

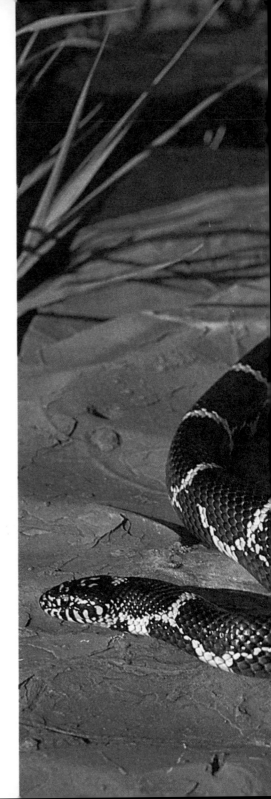

A New Year, New Babies

Baby snakes start their lives in different ways. Their mother may look for a warm, safe place to lay eggs—perhaps in a rotting log, a burrow or under leaves. Some kinds of snakes lay as few as 7 eggs while others lay as many as 60.

The eggs are white but are not brittle like chicken eggs. Instead, they feel like ping-pong balls, only a little softer. Inside the egg, the baby snake feeds on the yolk. When it is ready to hatch, it uses a small, sharp egg-tooth to chip its way through the shell. Soon after its work is done, the egg-tooth drops off.

Eastern Hog-nosed Snake hatching.

Other baby snakes live inside eggs which their mother carries inside her until they are ready to hatch. These babies also live on their egg's yolk. But the shells of their eggs are thin. They break open as they are pushed from the mother's body.

A few kinds of baby snakes are born live. They live inside a clear sac inside their mother's body. When they are born, their first job is to break out of their sac.

Young Eastern Milk Snake.

A Hard Start

Life is dangerous for a baby snake. Its mother leaves as soon as the eggs are laid or the babies are born. Many eggs and babies become food for other hunters, but many survive.

Baby snakes are like their parents in every way but size. For their first few years, they grow quickly. In places where the weather stays warm, young snakes grow all year. Snakes that hibernate do not grow during the winter, but they grow extra fast once the warm weather returns. In fact, snakes never really stop growing, although older snakes grow so slowly that you would hardly notice it.

Naturalists do not know how long snakes live in the wild. But they can guess because they have watched snakes in captivity. There, large snakes often live for more than twenty years and smaller ones often live to be ten or fifteen.

Special Words

Constrictor A snake that kills prey by squeezing it so it cannot breathe.

Egg tooth A hard point on the tip of a baby snake's nose which it uses to break its way out of its shell.

Fangs Long sharp hollow teeth through which venom flows in some snakes.

Heat sensors Organs that are specially sensitive to temperature.

Hibernaculum The place where a snake or group of snakes hibernates.

Hibernate To go into a deep sleep for the entire winter.

Mating season The time of year during which animals come together to produce young.

Musk A strong smelling substance produced by some animals.

Organs Parts of the body adapted for a particular vital function.

Prey An animal hunted by another animal for food.

Scales Thin, hard overlapping plates that protect a snake's skin.

Scutes The big rectangular scales on a snake's belly.

Venom Poisonous fluid produced by some snakes.

INDEX

Cover Photo: Brian Milne (First Light Associated Photographers)

Photo Credits: Norman Lightfoot (Eco-Art Productions), pages 4, 11, 20, 37, 41; Bill Ivy, pages 7, 8, 12, 15, 19, 24, 31, 34, 45; Tom W. Hall (Miller Services), pages 16, 28; Robert C. Simpson (Valan Photos), pages 23, 42; Dennis Schmidt (Valan Photos), page 27; E. Degginger (Miller Services), page 32; Gerhard Kahrmann (Valan Photos), page 38.